KT-558-276

Please return on or
before the last date
below.

the **information**

Teen Issues

TOBACCO

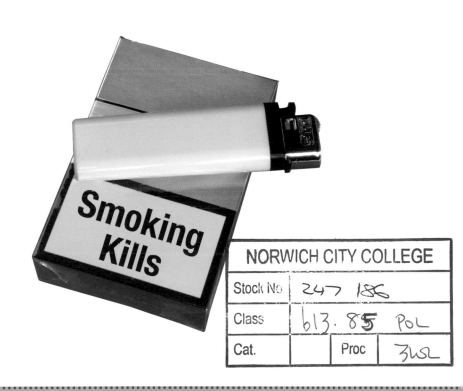

Smoking
Kills

NORWICH CITY COLLEGE		
Stock No	247 186	
Class	613.85 POL	
Cat.		Proc 3WL

Jim Pollard and Chloë Kent

Raintree

247 186

www.raintreepublishers.co.uk
Visit our website to find out more information about **Raintree** books.

To order:

 Phone 44 (0) 1865 888113

Send a fax to 44 (0) 1865 314091

Visit the Raintree Bookshop at **www.raintreepublishers.co.uk** to browse our catalogue and order online.

First published in Great Britain by
Raintree, Halley Court,
Jordan Hill, Oxford OX2 8EJ, part of
Harcourt Education.
Raintree is a registered trademark of Harcourt
Education Ltd.

© Harcourt Education Ltd 2004
First published in paperback in 2005
The moral right of the proprietor has been asserted.

All rights reserved. No part of this publication may be reproduced, stored in a retrieval system, or transmitted in any form or by any means, electronic, mechanical, photocopying, recording, or otherwise, without either the prior written permission of the publishers or a licence permitting restricted copying in the United Kingdom issued by the Copyright Licensing Agency Ltd, 90 Tottenham Court Road, London W1T 4LP (www.cla.co.uk).

Editorial: Charlotte Guillain and
Kate Buckingham
Design: Michelle Lisseter
and Tinstar Design Ltd (www.tinstar.co.uk)
Picture Research: Mica Brancic
Production: Jonathan Smith
Index: Indexing Specialists (UK) Ltd

Originated by Dot Gradations
Printed and bound in China by South China
Printing Company

ISBN 1 844 43143 6 (hardback)
08 07 06 05 04
10 9 8 7 6 5 4 3 2 1

ISBN 1 844 43150 9 (paperback)
09 08 07 06 05
10 9 8 7 6 5 4 3 2 1

British Library Cataloguing in Publication Data
Pollard, Jim
Tobacco
362.2'96
A full catalogue record for this book is available from the British Library.

Acknowledgements
The publishers would like to thank the following for permission to reproduce photographs: Alamy pp. 6–7, 10–11, 20, 34; Bubbles pp. 27, 30, 31, 37; Bubbles p. 43 (Chris Root); Bubbles pp. 5, 26 (Jennie Woodcock); Corbis pp. 4–5, 5, 7, 10, 11, 18, 18–19, 19, 22, 24–25, 25, 33, 35, 36, 39, 40–41, 42, 46–47, 46, 48, 49, 48–49, 51, 52–53; Getty pp. 26, 36–37 (Image Bank); Getty pp. 39, 40, 42–43, 44–45, 45 (PhotoDisc); Getty pp. 13, 21, 34–35 (Stone); Getty pp. 4, 38 (Taxi); Imagefile p. 12 (Powerstock); John Birdsall pp. 15, 41; Powerstock p. 29 (Superstock); Powerstock pp. 13, 14–15; Science Photo Library pp. 16, 16–17, 17, 21, 22–23, 23, 24, 30–31, 32–33, 47; Tudor Photography pp. i, 5, 6, 8, 8–9, 14, 28, 44, 50.

Cover photograph of cigarette packet reproduced with permission of Tudor Photography.

Every effort has been made to contact copyright holders of any material reproduced in this book. Any omissions will be rectified in subsequent printings if notice is given to the publishers.

The paper used to print this book comes from sustainable resources.

Disclaimer
All the Internet addresses (URLs) given in this book were valid at the time of going to press. However, due to the dynamic nature of the Internet, some addresses may have changed, or sites may have changed or ceased to exist since publication. While the author and Publishers regret any inconvenience this may cause readers, no responsibility for any such changes can be accepted by either the author or the publishers.

Contents

Any words appearing in the text in bold,
like this, are explained in the Glossary.
You can also look out for them in the 'In the
know' box at the bottom of each page.

Think of a number

So many smokers

There are 1.1 billion smokers in the world. Every day about 100,000 young people join them by becoming tobacco **addicts**.

The five countries with the most smokers are:
- China
- the USA
- Russia
- Japan
- Indonesia.

The five biggest tobacco companies in the world make about **4,269,000,000,000** cigarettes every year. If you laid all these cigarettes end to end they would stretch from the Earth to the Sun and back more than 22 times. That is a lot of cigarettes!

There are over 50 million smokers in the USA and over 200 million in Europe, but in these countries sales of cigarettes are falling. People in these countries know now that smoking is dangerous and it is becoming less fashionable. In poorer countries, people do not always know this and cigarette sales are going up. In China, more than 1,600 **billion** cigarettes are smoked each year.

addict   someone who finds it difficult or impossible to live without something

Where it comes from

Cigarettes are made from tobacco. Tobacco is a plant that is grown in many countries and is **exported** all around the world. Brazil, the USA, India and China produce two-thirds of the world's tobacco.

How people use it

Cigarettes are not the only way in which people use tobacco. It can be smoked in other ways – in a pipe or cigar. It can be chewed. It can even be sniffed up into the nose.

What it does

Smoking cigarettes and taking tobacco can affect you and the people around you in many ways. This book tells you the facts about tobacco and smoking so that you can make up your own mind.

Find out later...

What happens to your body when you smoke?

Why is smoking more dangerous when you are young?

How do you give up smoking or help someone else give up?

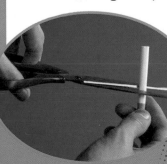

billion   one thousand million
exported   sold by one country to another

What is tobacco?

Big business

Tobacco is not just a plant, it is also a multi-**billion** dollar industry. The three biggest **multinational** firms are based in the USA, the UK and Japan. Tobacco made $88,000,000,000 in 1998.

There are many types of tobacco plant. Most have large green leaves and small coloured flowers. It is the leaves that people smoke. The leaves are cured, which means they are dried before they are rolled for smoking.

Cigarette tobacco is usually dried in the air. The tobacco for pipes, sniffing and chewing is often cured using a fire. Tobacco for sniffing is called snuff, but this is even more old-fashioned these days than other forms of tobacco.

The cured tobacco leaves are made into cigarettes and other tobacco products in factories.

Smoking is highly addictive, don't start

fragrance   smell

Nothing new

People have grown tobacco for thousands of years. The Huron Native Americans saw it as a gift from their god, the Great Spirit. South American pots from the 11th century are decorated with pictures of people smoking.

Whether we smoke it, chew it or sniff it, tobacco does not look very tasty. That is what Christopher Columbus thought when he landed in North America in 1492. His diary says that the natives gave him 'fruit, wooden spears, and certain dried leaves which gave off a distinct **fragrance**.' The sailors ate the fruit but threw the leaves away.

Chewing tobacco

Chewing tobacco is common in some parts of the USA and also in many Muslim countries where smoking may be frowned on for religious reasons.

◄ This tobacco farm is in Malaysia.

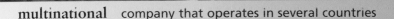

multinational   company that operates in several countries

What is in a cigarette?

Cigarettes contain the following ingredients:

What else is in it?

Most of the additives put in cigarettes are the sort of chemicals that are added to food and drink. They may be harmless by themselves, but when they are burned and mixed with other chemicals they can become **toxic**.

▼ Substances added to cigarettes include alcohol, vinegar, apple juice and walnuts.

Blend of tobaccos – some tobacco plants are higher in **nicotine**, some smell nicer than others.

Fillers – these are made of the stems and other waste parts of tobacco plants. When there is more filler, there is usually less tar.

Moisturisers – these keep the cigarettes fresh in the packet.

Sugars – these make the smoke easier to take down.

Flavourings – these can include chocolate and vanilla.

Filter – this traps some smoke and cools the rest.

Paper – thinner paper with more **pores** lets in more air and may reduce the amount of smoke that reaches the smoker's **lungs**.

lungs   part of the body used for breathing
nicotine   addictive, colourless chemical

Legal or illegal?

If you are over 18 years old, which of these drugs are **legal** and which are **illegal**?

- Heroin
- Alcohol
- Caffeine
- Paracetamol
- Tobacco
- Cannabis

Tobacco is legal all over the world. But this does not mean it is safe. Far more people are killed by the legal drugs alcohol and tobacco than by the illegal ones heroin and cannabis.

What is safe is much more complicated than what is legal. It is illegal for you to take heroin yourself, but it is quite legal for a doctor to give it to you as a painkiller. Paracetamol is legal, but if you take too many tablets, they could kill you.

Legal but bad for you

Caffeine is a legal drug. It is found in coffee, tea and cola drinks. Alcohol is legal too. But like tobacco, both these drugs can be bad for your health.

▷ ▷ ▷ ▷ ▷ ▷ ▷ ▷ ▷

Turn to page 20 to find out how smoking affects your taste buds.

pore tiny hole
toxic poisonous

Why smoke?

TRUE OR FALSE?

'Tobacco cannot be that dangerous. If it was, they would not be allowed to advertise it.'

FALSE

Tobacco is the only product sold legally that can damage your health even when it is used in the correct way.

Tobacco has been popular in Europe and the USA for hundreds of years. Most of us know someone who smokes. People start smoking for all sorts of reasons. Until recently, it was a pretty normal part of everyday life.

Nobody knew that smoking was bad for you until less than 50 years ago. Some people even thought that smoking was good for your health. Smoking was seen as grown-up and glamorous. Famous film stars and musicians were often photographed smoking. People who could not afford the clothes, the cars or the houses in the photos could afford the same brand of cigarettes. It is not surprising that smoking became popular.

Advertising

Tobacco has always been advertised a lot, often using famous celebrities. For example, Ronald Reagan, the actor who became a US president, used to advertise cigarettes.

► All four members of The Beatles used to smoke.

sponsorship   when a company helps to pay for something in return for advertising

Seeing film stars with cigarettes made smoking seem very fashionable. Today, some actors and actresses still smoke. This helps the tobacco companies because now it is much more difficult for them to advertise in the normal way. In 2003, all 192 countries in the World Health Organization agreed to limit the advertising, marketing and sale of tobacco products.

Sponsorship is another way of making smoking look good. Tobacco companies are allowed to continue to sponsor motor racing until 2006.

The film factor

Research in the USA showed that teenagers who had seen films with smoking in them were three times more likely to have tried cigarettes.

Some reasons teens start to smoke

All my friends do.

I didn't want to be left out.

It looked fun.

I wanted to know what it was like.

Teenage smokers

Most people start smoking when they are teenagers. One reason may be because it looks grown-up. Young people are more likely to smoke if the adults they live with smoke.

But when you are a teenager, people of your own age are just as big an influence on what you do. Smoking can make people feel part of a group. Nervous or shy people say that smoking gives them something to do. Offering someone a cigarette can be a way of starting a conversation.

Advertising also works very well with young people. In the USA, 86 per cent of teenage smokers use the three most widely-advertised brands.

charcoal   burned wood

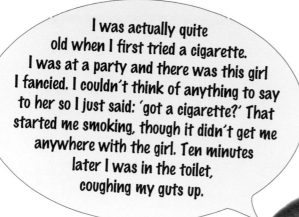

I was actually quite old when I first tried a cigarette. I was at a party and there was this girl I fancied. I couldn't think of anything to say to her so I just said: 'got a cigarette?' That started me smoking, though it didn't get me anywhere with the girl. Ten minutes later I was in the toilet, coughing my guts up.

After my first cigarette…

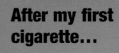

I had to go outside for some fresh air.

Jen, 16

The other girls who used to smoke always seemed more interesting but it wasn't really that. I think I started smoking because everyone said 'don't do it'. I didn't believe that something on sale legally in a shop could be as dangerous as people said.

I thought it would taste of mint because it said menthol on the box, but it tasted more like **charcoal**.

Jamal, 16

The effects of tobacco

Wherever your first cigarette comes from and wherever you smoke it, everybody agrees that smoking is horrible to start with.

I had my first cigarette last night. I felt sick.

Yuck i had my first kiss last nite. It was gr8!

My first chew

We started chewing tobacco because it was much easier to hide than cigarettes. The first time, it tasted disgusting. My friend accidentally swallowed his and was sick for hours.

My first cigarette

When I smoked my first cigarette, I thought I'd burn my tongue. I coughed even though I didn't **inhale**. It makes you feel sick. It makes your head spin. But I thought it made me look cool too. My throat was sore as sandpaper the next day and I didn't have another go for a couple of years.

It makes me feel good

Although smoking makes people feel ill at first, they often carry on because they like it. People enjoy smoking when they start to get more of the good feelings and fewer of the problems.

The trouble is that the **nicotine** in tobacco is very powerful. It can take just a few cigarettes for your body to become dependent on nicotine. Then you need nicotine just to be able to feel normal.

Once the drug is in control and not you, it can be very difficult to stop. Two smokers in every three would like to give up if only they could.

Q&A

Q Are cigarettes really more dangerous than heroin?

A Some people think so. Smoking kills more people and some people say it is even harder to give up smoking than to quit heroin.

Nicotine is a poison. Just 60 milligrams of pure nicotine would kill you within minutes.

What happens when you smoke?

Smoking affects your body beyond the good and bad feelings you have when you **inhale** the smoke. Altogether there are more than 4000 chemicals in cigarette smoke. They can have all sorts of effects.

The main chemicals are:
- **Nicotine:** A very addictive, colourless liquid that is poisonous in larger amounts.
- **Tar:** A brown, treacle-like substance that contains well-known poisons like arsenic, cyanide and formaldehyde.
- **Carbon monoxide:** The same poisonous gas that comes out of car exhausts.

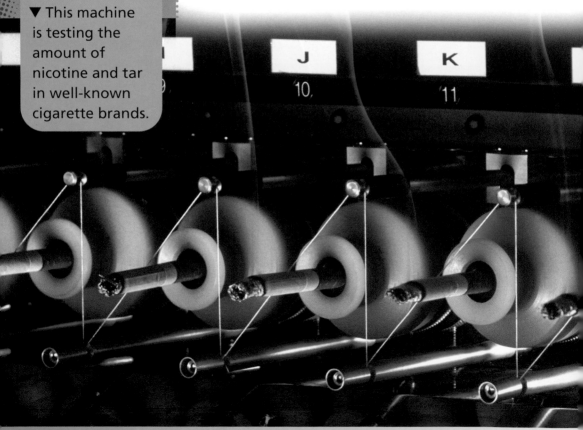

▼ This machine is testing the amount of nicotine and tar in well-known cigarette brands.

blood pressure pressure of the blood going around the body; high blood pressure is dangerous

When you smoke, these chemicals affect your body in the following ways:

Brain	After 10 seconds, the nicotine in the smoke reaches your brain. It sends a buzz through the body's **central nervous system**. This is the bit most smokers like, but it only lasts for a few seconds.
Eyes	Smoke gets in your eyes and stings.
Lungs	Your **lungs** must work harder to deal with the smoke that you are filling them with. You start breathing more heavily and more deeply. Because of this, even more damage is caused by the chemicals in the smoke.
Heart	Your **heart rate** goes up by as much as 30 per cent in 10 minutes. Your **blood pressure** also increases. This makes your heart work harder and increases the risk of a heart attack over time.
Blood	Carbon monoxide in the smoke mixes with your blood. This makes it more difficult for the blood to carry oxygen around your body. If your blood does not have enough oxygen, you will feel tired.

▲To take your pulse, put your finger just to the left of centre on the underside of your left wrist. Count how many beats you feel over a minute.

Take your pulse

You can measure your heart rate by taking your pulse. The average pulse for a younger teenager is 75 to 90 beats a minute. Girls usually have higher heart rates than boys.

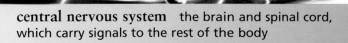

central nervous system   the brain and spinal cord, which carry signals to the rest of the body

> **'When you are young, you can play sport even if you smoke.'**

It is true that you can play sport, but it is a fact that you will not be as good at it. The **carbon monoxide** in smoke makes it more difficult for oxygen to move around in your blood. Your **lungs** are less **efficient**, too. You will get tired sooner and take longer to recover.

The downside

Smokers notice the effects of tobacco even more when they try to get their body to do something like sport or dancing. This is what happened to Leroy. He had been trying to get into the athletics team for years.

> I finally got picked for the cross-country team. It was what I'd always wanted. For a while it was fantastic, but then the smoking got me. Suddenly, I wasn't beating my personal best all the time any more. In fact, I was getting slower. After a race I'd cough like anything and felt half-dead.

efficient   good at doing its job

Image-Sticks

What do you think of this idea for a new product?

Buy new Image-Sticks

We guarantee they'll make a big difference to how you look:

- **your teeth and fingers will be yellow**
- **your hair will have that just-burned smell of an old bonfire**
- **your skin will dry up and wrinkle so you will look really old**
- **your breath will be as fresh as a used ashtray**

What do you think? Image-Sticks do not exist. Who would buy them?

Bad taste

❝ There's one thing that's worse than kissing her after she's had a smoke. It's kissing her after she's sprayed that freshener in her mouth or eaten a mint. Does she really think it makes a difference? It's still like kissing an ashtray – a sickly, sweet, mint-flavoured ashtray. ❞

No taste

If you enjoy tasting delicious food then it is best not to smoke or chew tobacco. It damages your sense of taste and sense of smell.

▼ Smokers cannot taste their food very well so they often eat too much salt just to get some flavour.

Smoking can damage your skin

Cigarette smoke makes it more difficult for the blood to carry oxygen around the whole body, including the skin. Without enough oxygen, the skin is less stretchy so that it wrinkles more easily. The smoke that is breathed out makes this worse because it dries the skin even more. That is why older smokers often have greyish, creased skin with thick lines around their eyes and mouth. Smoking may also **encourage** hair to turn grey or fall out. Many smokers look older than they really are. Smokers in their 40s often have as many wrinkles on their faces as **non-smokers** in their 60s.

encourage   help

Beauty tip

Jenny gave up smoking when she was 18.

> You want to know the secret of my great skin? It's not the moisturiser or the foundation — it's the smoking. I gave up six months ago. What a difference! You can't repair damage that's already done, but at least this face cream might work now.

▲ The yellow-black staining around these teeth is from cigarette tar.

Tar damage

It is the **tar** in tobacco that turns your teeth yellow. It also damages your gums. This means that smokers tend to lose more teeth and spend more time at the dentist.

> It was looking at my mother that made me give up. She showed me a picture of her as a girl and she looked exactly like me. Now she's got bags under her eyes and skin like cheap cardboard. She's only 20 years older than I am but she smokes 20 cigarettes a day.

non-smoker someone who does not smoke

Tobacco and your body

Over time, smoking does not just stain your fingers and teeth, it damages almost every part of your body. At least 43 of the chemicals in tobacco smoke can cause cancer.

You can clean your teeth or wash your hands, but some of the problems inside your body are more difficult to put right. Some of them need drastic treatment.

▼ This man had to have his toe amputated because his heavy smoking meant blood was not flowing properly around his body.

Forecast

The World Health Organization believes that by 2030, 10 million people will die every year from smoking. This is more than half the population of Australia!

Half of all the teenagers who are smoking today will die from diseases caused by tobacco if they carry on smoking.

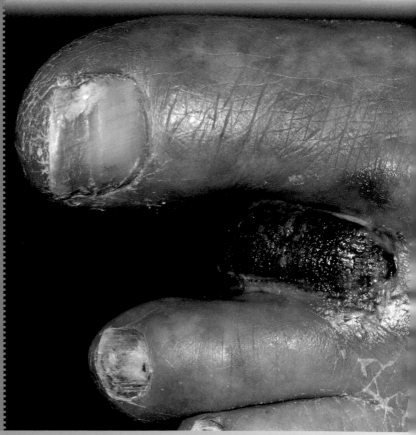

amputate   cut off

Here are some of the ways in which smoking can affect your body:

Brain	At least one-third of strokes are caused by smoking. A stroke happens when brain cells suddenly die because the blood in the brain is not circulating properly.
Lungs	Lung cancer causes the most cancer deaths in the world.
Throat	90 per cent of throat and mouth cancers are caused by smoking or chewing tobacco.
Heart	Because a smoker's heart has to work harder, a cigarette smoker is two to three times more likely to have a heart attack than a **non-smoker**.
Limbs	About 2000 arms and legs are **amputated** in the UK because of diseases caused by smoking. This most often affects men between 20 and 40.
Fertility	Smoking can affect the **fertility** of both men and women.

Q How can smoking cause you to lose a leg?

A It is because smoking stops the blood from circulating properly. In cases where the blood cannot circulate in your leg, cells die and your leg may need to be amputated.

fertility   ability to have children

Lung damage

Emphysema is a serious **lung** disease. Many smokers suffer from it.

Our lungs are full of millions of tiny air sacs called **alveoli**. Alveoli help oxygen into the body and help carbon dioxide out. Smoke makes this more difficult and can even make the alveoli burst in long-term smokers. The fewer alveoli you have, the worse your lungs will work. This damage can never be repaired.

Over time, the body of someone with emphysema becomes desperate for oxygen. Every single breath is difficult and painful. Even very simple exercise, such as walking up a step, can become almost impossible.

Heart attacks

The UK has one of the worst records in the world for deaths from heart disease. Many of these deaths are caused by smoking. Being a smoker immediately increases your chance of having a heart attack.

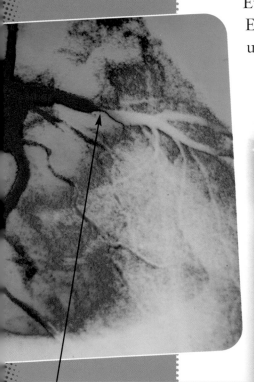

The narrowing of the **artery** in this smoker is likely to cause a heart attack.

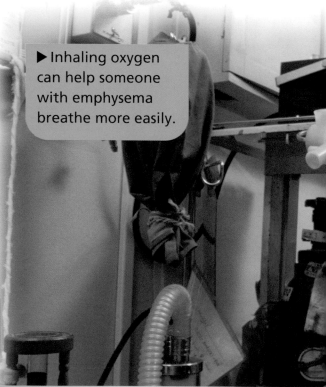

▶ Inhaling oxygen can help someone with emphysema breathe more easily.

   alveoli   tiny air sacs in the lungs

Cancer

Lung cancer also nearly always affects smokers. Four out of five lung cancer deaths are caused by smoking.

The younger you are when you start smoking, the greater your risk of developing lung cancer. Smoking when you are a teenager can cause permanent changes in your lungs that increase the risk of lung cancer forever – even if you stop smoking when you are older.

The longer you smoke, the greater the risk of lung cancer. Someone who smokes ten cigarettes a day for twenty years is at more risk than someone who smokes twenty a day for ten years.

One too many

‘ But I only smoke a couple a day. ’

Even people who smoke one or two cigarettes a day are still two to three times more likely to die of heart disease than people who do not smoke. But the risk increases as you smoke more. Young men who smoke 25 or more cigarettes a day are fifteen times as likely to die from heart disease as **non-smokers** of the same age.

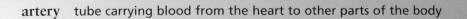

artery   tube carrying blood from the heart to other parts of the body

Smoking can damage your sex life

Some people think that smoking looks sexy. But in fact, smokers are making themselves a lot less sexy. Smoking can actually damage your sex organs. It can also cause sexual problems later in life.

A man gets an **erection** as the result of blood flowing into his penis. Smoking interferes with blood flow, so male smokers may find it difficult to get an erection. This is sometimes called **impotence**. Male smokers are twice as likely to suffer from impotence as men who do not smoke.

Male smokers also produce fewer **sperm** and their sperm are less healthy.

Dog breath

I know that smoking reduces blood flow so your penis is smaller when it's erect. But that's the least of my problems at the moment. My girlfriend says my breath is like a dog's and she won't even kiss me until I stop smoking.

impotence   inability to get an erection

Pete's problem

Pete was depressed, so he wrote to his girlfriend's magazine.

hope that helps and don't worry.

Dear Jo,
I've been having trouble making love with my girlfriend for a few months now. I'm interested but my body isn't. Now my girlfriend isn't interested in sex either. I smoke and she says it's the smell that puts her off.

Dear Pete,
Have you thought that your girlfriend might be trying to drop a hint that you should stop smoking? Perhaps she knows about the research that found that men who smoked more than 20 cigarettes daily had a 60 per cent higher risk of erection problems than men who never smoked. So stop smoking and start enjoying yourself.

Dear Jo,
Could you please help m

▲ Women smokers find it more difficult to get pregnant than **non-smokers**.

Lower fertility

A woman smoker is 20 per cent less likely to get pregnant than a non-smoker. Even breathing other people's cigarette smoke can damage a woman's **fertility**.

sperm special cells produced by male sex organs that join with a female egg to make a new living thing

Smoking can damage everything

The three main killers of smokers are **lung cancer**, other lung diseases and heart disease. But smokers are at greater risk of many other long-term health problems too.

TRUE OR FALSE?

'You can easily smoke now and give up when you are older.'

FALSE

It will only get more difficult to give up. Nicotine is as addictive as heroin or cocaine.

Arthritis
This makes your joints very painful – a long term smoking habit can put you at risk of developing this.

Asthma
You are more likely to develop **asthma** if you spend a lot of time in contact with tobacco smoke.

Back pain
New research shows that smoking may increase the risk of lower back problems.

Bowel problems
Smoking is thought to irritate Crohn's disease, a condition that causes painful **inflammation** in the **intestines**.

Diabetes
The risk of **diabetes** can be reduced by leading a healthier lifestyle including giving up smoking.

◄ ◄ ◄ ◄ ◄ ◄ ◄ ◄ ◄
Go to page 21 to see the damage smoking can do to teeth.

diabetes   disease where sugar and starch are not absorbed into the body properly

Eye problems

A study carried out in 1998 showed that nearly all eye diseases, some of which result in blindness, are made worse by smoking.

Flu

Smokers are likely to get illnesses such as colds and flu that hang on for longer than they would in a **non-smoker**.

Gum disease and tooth loss

Smoking is now widely thought to hide the early signs of **gum disease** because **nicotine** reduces bleeding in the gums (an early warning of gum disease).

Osteoporosis

This is a disease that means your bones break easily. Smoking is thought to put you at higher risk of developing the disease.

Pneumonia

Exposure to tobacco smoke is linked with an increased risk of **respiratory** infections, such as **pneumonia**.

Tuberculosis

By damaging the lung's defences, smoking is believed to increase the danger that a minor infection may get out of control and cause **tuberculosis**.

Every time a smoker lights a cigarette, they are increasing their risk of developing at least one of these problems.

True or False?

'**Low-tar cigarettes are just as dangerous as high-tar.**'

TRUE

The evidence shows that people who smoke low-**tar** cigarettes smoke more and **inhale** harder to get the same buzz. In fact, some types of lung cancer are higher among smokers of low-tar cigarettes.

---

inflammation painful redness or swelling

You think it will never happen to you

Hospitals today are full of older and middle-aged people fighting against diseases and illnesses caused by smoking. When they were young, perhaps they did not know how dangerous smoking was. Or perhaps they knew and took the risk anyway. They probably thought that **lung** cancer or heart disease only happened to other people.

'It doesn't take long to get addicted to tobacco.'

TRUE

It can take just a couple of days. US research found that young people get **addicted** to **nicotine** more quickly than adults, because their brains are still developing.

addicted   unable to live without something

Frank's story

It is easy to think that the problems will happen to someone else and that you will be OK. Frank thought the same thing.

When I started smoking I was 14. People didn't really know that smoking was dangerous then. I only started thinking about the dangers when my dad died. He was only 64. Not even old enough to retire.

My dad used to smoke 20 cigarettes a day. By the time he died it was too late for me to give up. I would give up for a couple of days and I managed a week once, but I never stuck at it.

I suppose I told myself that because smoking had killed my dad, it couldn't kill me too. That just wouldn't be fair. But life doesn't work like that, does it? The doctors say I've got two years to live. I'll be even younger than my dad was when he died.

I wish someone had told me what a chance I was taking when I was 14.

▲ Why not do some research? Talk to older people about the smokers they know.

Family history

Do you have older relatives who smoke and have health problems? We get our looks from our parents and grandparents. We get our lungs and hearts from them, too.

What about smokeless tobacco?

Many people think that chewing tobacco is safer than smoking it. This is not true. All forms of tobacco are dangerous.

Of course, there is no dangerous smoke if you chew tobacco, but the tobacco itself is in far closer contact with the body. The **nicotine** in chewing tobacco increases the **heart rate** and **blood pressure** – just like other forms of tobacco.

▼ Tongue cancer is often linked to people who regularly chew tobacco.

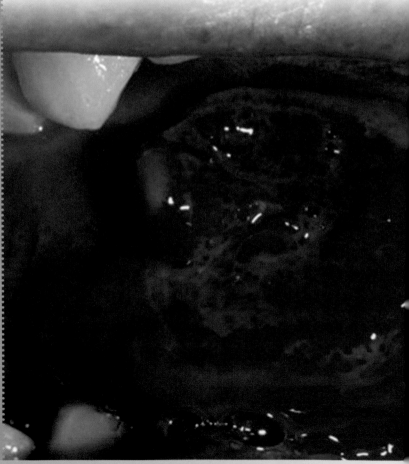

TRUE OR FALSE?

'Smokeless tobacco is not anti-social because it does not harm other people like cigarettes do.'

TRUE

But the cost of treating the illnesses caused by all types of tobacco is very high. It harms whoever has to pay, whether it is your family or the **tax-payer**. And that is pretty anti-social. The USA spends about $75 **billion** a year on treating illnesses caused by tobacco.

Chewing tobacco can cause mouth, cheek, tongue, throat and stomach cancer. Smokeless tobacco users are 50 times more likely to get these sorts of cancers than non-users.

Chewing tobacco also causes stained teeth, bad breath, bleeding gums and mouth sores.

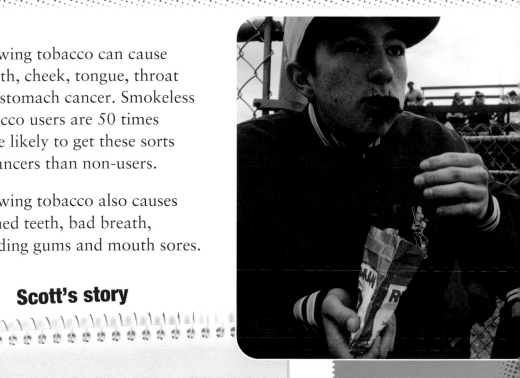

Scott's story

I started chewing tobacco like everyone else. It made me feel like an adult.

After you've been chewing a while you get so you always want something in your mouth to chew. It's really hard to stop, even though your mouth is sore all the time. My tongue became numb and I couldn't eat properly. I knew someone who had mouth cancer. They said that he could have been saved if he'd seen a doctor sooner. So I saw my doctor and now I may have to have an operation on my tongue. They say I should be able to talk OK afterwards. Hope so.

Addicted to salt
There is so much salt in chewing tobacco that users can become desperate for salt as well as nicotine. Too much salt is bad for the heart and most of us already eat more than we need.

Second-hand smoking

Second-hand smoking

Second-hand smokers breathe two types of smoke. Mainstream smoke is the smoke that has already been **inhaled** by the smoker. Secondary smoke is the smoke from the end of the burning cigarette.

The most dangerous gases are mainly in the secondary smoke, because this smoke has not passed through the filter or the smoker's **lungs**. Nearly 85 per cent of the smoke in a room is secondary smoke.

You do not need to smoke to suffer the effects of smoking. Breathing in somebody else's tobacco smoke can also be dangerous. This is called second-hand smoking or passive smoking.

People who live with a smoker have a higher risk of getting **lung** cancer than people who do not live with a smoker. Children who live with smokers get colds and flu and other illnesses more often than children who live with **non-smokers**. Children who live with smokers are also less healthy when they grow up.

More and more public places such as cinemas and restaurants do not allow smoking because of the dangers of second-hand smoking. Many offices and factories also ban smoking.

Smoking affects your social life

Vidya and Anita were emailing each other about Sara's party.

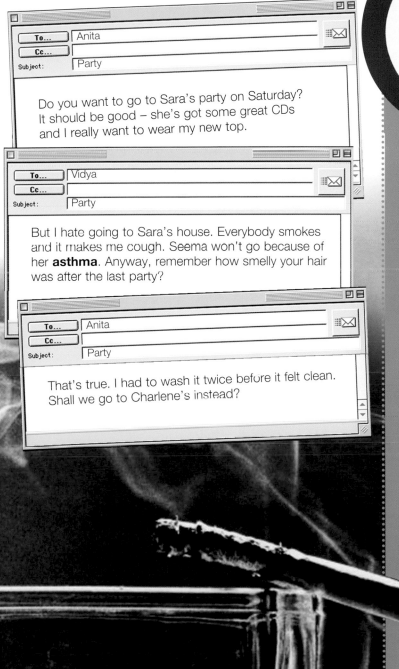

To... Anita
Cc...
Subject: Party

Do you want to go to Sara's party on Saturday?
It should be good – she's got some great CDs
and I really want to wear my new top.

To... Vidya
Cc...
Subject: Party

But I hate going to Sara's house. Everybody smokes
and it makes me cough. Seema won't go because of
her **asthma**. Anyway, remember how smelly your hair
was after the last party?

To... Anita
Cc...
Subject: Party

That's true. I had to wash it twice before it felt clean.
Shall we go to Charlene's instead?

Do you mind?

What do you think?
Do you mind
breathing in other
people's smoke?
Should smoking be
banned in public
places? Or should
people have the
right to smoke
anywhere they
want to?

Risking everything

Pregnant women who smoke are more likely to have a **miscarriage** or **still birth**. Their babies are usually smaller. Most of the damage happens in the last six months of pregnancy, so giving up at any time in the first three months will help.

Why me?

Every year thousands of people become ill and die from diseases caused by smoking, even though they have never smoked.

Rachel and Jamie's mum has recently had a heart attack:

> I've never smoked. Never even had a puff. But the doctors say that the heart disease I've got is typical of smokers. It's not such a mystery really. My husband used to smoke and now my daughter Rachel does. I used to work in a really smoky office, too. I've been breathing other people's smoke for years.

miscarriage   when a pregnancy ends before the unborn baby has developed enough to live

The charity ASH estimate that every year in the UK about 12,000 non-smokers get heart disease from second-hand smoking. I must be one of them. Rachel feels terrible about what's happened. She keeps saying that if only she'd known she would never have smoked. She thought she was only risking her own life. Now, she keeps asking the doctors if my heart operation is going to work. Well, of course, they can't say for certain, can they?

The only good thing is that my son says he's never going to smoke. Well, I suppose if seeing your mum having heart surgery doesn't put you off, nothing will.

Trying to stop

' I tried to give up when I got pregnant but I couldn't. I felt awful because I thought that most of the damage would be when the baby was smallest. But the doctor told me that the main problems were caused later on. So now I'm trying to give up again. '

still birth   giving birth to a baby that has died in the womb
surgery   operation in hospital

Giving up smoking

More for your money

More for your money

❝I gave up smoking as my New Year's resolution last year. I put all the money I would have spent on cigarettes in a box and this year in the sales I blew the lot on clothes! Thinking about what I could buy kept me going through the year when I was tempted to have a smoke.❞

Giving up smoking is difficult, but every year thousands of people manage it.

Here are ten of the most common reasons for giving up:

- to be healthier
- to live longer
- to have more money for other things
- to have more energy and feel fitter
- to feel more attractive through smelling nicer and having better skin, hair and teeth
- to be able to enjoy food and drink again
- to feel in control and stop worrying about when and where you are next going to be able to smoke
- to stop helping big tobacco companies make bigger profits
- to not damage the environment with tobacco farms and factories
- to have a healthy baby.

How much does smoking cost?

The amount of money the average smoker spends each year on smoking could buy:

- an all-expenses-paid holiday in the sun for two
- the world's fastest personal computer
- 10 portable MP3 players
- 64 computer games
- 100 CDs
- 230 cinema tickets
- 320 lipsticks.

Smoking costs the country a lot, too. Researchers estimate that in the UK, treating diseases caused by smoking costs about £1.5 **billion** a year. That could buy nearly 100 million CDs. Or some new hospitals.

What do you think?

There is a high tax on tobacco. Smokers pay for their addiction.

True. But that money could be spent on better things. Look how much the rest of us pay to look after smokers' health. If it wasn't for smokers there'd be smaller waiting lists for operations.

◀ Give up smoking and you could have a fantastic holiday with the money you save!

I want to be able to taste what I'm cooking.

I want to be able to concentrate on my work without having to keep taking smoking breaks.

Feel better

If you want to **encourage** someone to give up smoking, tell them that they will be healthier within just 20 minutes of stopping.

It may be tough to quit, but the benefits start straight away and keep on getting bigger and better. You can start putting right any damage smoking has done to your body from the moment you stub out your last cigarette.

There are people who can hardly move because smoking has damaged their health so much. They often say that smoking is the only thing they have left in life. In other words, it is hard to give up smoking before it ruins your life, but it is even harder afterwards.

Think about it...

20 minutes after stopping smoking
Blood pressure and **heart rate** are back to normal.

After 8 hours
Oxygen in the blood is back to normal. Chances of a heart attack start to fall. Sleep improves.

After 24 hours
Carbon monoxide is now out of the body and **lungs** start to clear.

After 48 hours
Nicotine is now out of the body. Sense of taste improves. You smell nicer.

After 72 hours
Breathing is much easier. Energy levels increase.

After 2 to 12 weeks
Blood circulation improves.

After one year
Risk of heart disease has halved. Risk of lung cancer is falling.

After 15 years
Risk of heart disease is back to the same as someone who has never smoked.

I don't want to smell like an ashtray.

I don't want to kill myself or anyone else.

I don't like the thought of being **addicted** to a drug.

Give up, get fit

John was saving up for a bike

Look at that bike, it's great.

If you gave up smoking you could buy that in two months.

More questions

Here are some common questions people ask about giving up smoking.

Q Does smoking get more and more dangerous if you smoke more and more cigarettes?

A Yes, and it is pretty easy to work out the risk. If you smoke 20 cigarettes a day, you are 20 times more likely to get **lung** cancer than a **non-smoker**.

Q Does age matter?

A Yes. Smoking is most damaging when you are young. Your body is still developing when you are a teenager. Someone who starts smoking at 15 has a higher risk of lung cancer than someone who starts at 25.

Q I've heard that each cigarette takes five minutes off your life. Is that right?

A Pretty much. On average, non-smokers live about eight years longer than smokers.

Q Will I put on weight if I stop smoking?

A Maybe. Maybe not. Some people even lose weight. If you do gain weight it probably will not last for long – unless you were a bit underweight to begin with. Non-fattening alternatives to smoking include chewing gum and drinking water and, of course, exercise. Exercise will also take your mind off smoking.

It's easier to stop now

If you are a teenage smoker, now is the best time to give it up. The longer you wait, the more **addicted** you will become and then stopping is a lot harder. You may really want a cigarette at first, but it gets easier after just three or four days. Don't give in – think of the money you are saving.

► Your doctor can help you to work out how to quit.

'You don't have to give up completely. You can just cut down on the amount you smoke.'

FALSE

You will still be **addicted** to **nicotine**, so eventually you will start smoking more again.

How do you give up smoking?

Giving up smoking is tough. But it is not impossible.

Some people just stop. Others set a date and tell everyone they are going to do it. It is a good idea to have the support of your family and friends, as you will probably be a bit grumpy for a while.

It is even harder to give up if all your friends still smoke. Try to get some of them to give up with you. That way you can **encourage** and support each other.

Make a plan

Think about what times of day you smoke and change your routine to avoid those moments. For example, if you always smoke walking home from school, get the bus or ride a bike instead. Throw away all your cigarettes so you do not get tempted.

You can do it

Claudia has recently given up smoking. She sent this email to her brother.

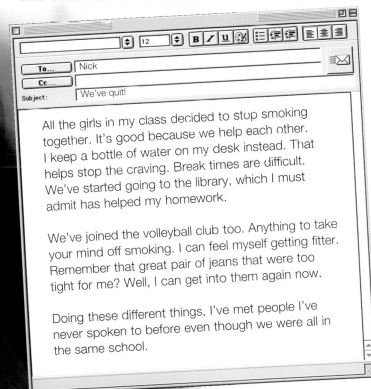

To... Nick
Cc...
Subject: We've quit!

All the girls in my class decided to stop smoking together. It's good because we help each other. I keep a bottle of water on my desk instead. That helps stop the craving. Break times are difficult. We've started going to the library, which I must admit has helped my homework.

We've joined the volleyball club too. Anything to take your mind off smoking. I can feel myself getting fitter. Remember that great pair of jeans that were too tight for me? Well, I can get into them again now.

Doing these different things, I've met people I've never spoken to before even though we were all in the same school.

How much?

You can work out how much you spend on tobacco each year.

price of pack of 20

x number you smoke per day

x 20

This will give you a rough total which even allows for the price of cigarettes going up a little in the future.

How do you help someone else give up?

If you are trying to help someone to give up smoking, here are some of the things they can try.

Cigarette smokers are **addicted** to **nicotine**, so getting the nicotine from somewhere else can stop them needing to smoke. There are nicotine chewing-gums, nicotine patches to stick on your skin, nicotine inhalers, nicotine nose sprays and nicotine **lozenges**.

A doctor is the best person to advise someone on which of these to use. Doctors can also prescribe drugs which can help people to give up smoking.

An adult could also try **acupuncture** or **hypnosis**. The local health food shop can suggest other alternatives.

Something to chew on

There are also alternatives to chewing tobacco, how about chewing mints or gum instead?

acupuncture   traditional Chinese treatment using needles

Be patient and positive

Jon has been helping his mum give up smoking.

Mum's been a right pain since she gave up smoking. I chucked out all the ashtrays and lighters like she asked me to and now she says the house looks empty without them. I make her put the money she's saving in a bowl. It's nearly full already. She could spend the money on ornaments if she thinks the house is so bare.

I keep telling her she looks better, too. It's no lie. She used to have grey skin, but not now. She's **paranoid** about putting on weight, so every time she starts moaning I give her a carrot to chew on.

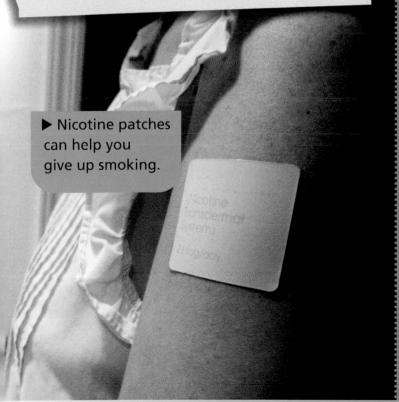

▶ Nicotine patches can help you give up smoking.

TRUE OR FALSE?

'**Sticking a needle in your ear can help stop you smoking.**'

TRUE

But only if it is done by a professional. Acupuncturists use needles in certain points in the ear to help treat addictions to tobacco.

hypnosis   sleep-like state that someone puts you into so they can affect the things you think and do

Tobacco and the law

Age limits

In the UK, it is against the law to sell tobacco to someone under 16 years old.
In Australia, you have to be 18 years old to buy tobacco.

Tobacco companies say that their adverts are not designed to make people start smoking but to **encourage** people who already smoke to change brand. These days, not many people believe them. When a law banning cigarette advertising was introduced in the UK in 2003, the health minister said: 'Advertising works; smoking kills. Today, we are breaking the link between the two.'

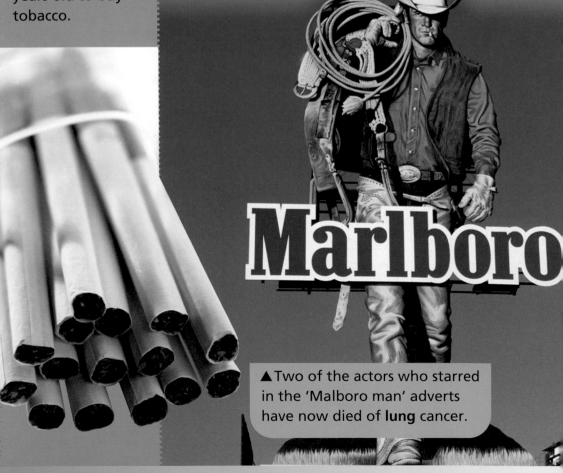

Marlboro

▲ Two of the actors who starred in the 'Malboro man' adverts have now died of **lung** cancer.

No smoking

More and more places are now banning smoking – offices and factories, bars and restaurants, buses and trains, cinemas and theatres. Several states and cities in the USA, Canada and Australia have banned smoking in all public places. More and more people support these bans.

6 It's really good now that this is a non-smoking place. The food's always been good but I never used to come in because the smoke spoiled the taste. 9

6 Even though I smoke I support the ban on smoking in restaurants. I moan about having to stand in the street every time I want a cigarette, but it means I'm smoking less. And the atmosphere's much better inside now. 9

Make it illegal?

Some people think the law should be even tougher. What do you think? Should tobacco be banned?

▶ The US government's main health advisor, Dr Richard Carmona, says nobody should be able to buy tobacco at all.

Raising the age

In the USA, you generally have to be 18 years old to buy tobacco. But in some states you must be 19, and some states are thinking about raising the age limit to 21.

49

The future

What is the future of the tobacco industry? Scientists first saw that smoking caused serious diseases like lung cancer in the 1950s. But for many years the tobacco companies said this research was not true. They also said that **nicotine** was not addictive.

Paying for the damage

In the 1990s, people who had worked for the tobacco companies began to admit that for a long time the companies had known that tobacco was dangerous. In 1998, the tobacco companies paid $206 **billion compensation** to 46 US states to make up for the damage they had done to the public's health. They may have to pay out even more.

TRUE OR FALSE?

'Warnings on cigarette packs do not work.'

FALSE

In the UK, bigger, more serious warnings about the dangers of smoking were put on cigarette packets. As a result, telephone helplines got more calls from people wanting to stop smoking.

Smoking Kills

compensation   money paid to try to make up for something bad that has happened to someone

US Government sues leading tobacco companies

The US government is suing the world's leading tobacco companies for $289 billion for not telling the truth when selling their cigarettes.

The government claims that the companies knew that tobacco was addictive and dangerous but did not admit this in their advertising. The US government has also accused the companies of continuing to deliberately try to sell cigarettes to teenagers.

The plain truth

Is this the cigarette packet of the future? They may be covered in warnings but with no advertising or branding at all apart from the name of the company.

What about you?

Whether you decide to smoke or not is up to you. Whatever you choose to do, remember that there are more unhappy smokers than happy smokers. How do we know this? Because in surveys, 65 to 70 per cent of smokers always say they would give up if they could. That is probably why most teenagers choose not to smoke.

SMOKING KILLS

SMOKING KILLS

Lucky Star

Smoking regularly can cause:

- **Heart attacks**
- **Lung cancer**
- **Impotence**
- **Ageing skin**

SMOKING KILLS

Find out more

Organizations

The Australian Drug Foundation

The Australian Drug Foundation has a wide range of information on all aspects of drugs, their effects and their legal position in Australia.
www.adf.org.au

Ash

Information for people concerned about smoking, whether they are smokers, secondary-smokers or friends of smokers.
www.ash.org

Lifebytes

A fun website that gives young people information to help them make their own choices about their life.
www.lifebytes.gov.uk

Quit

A national charity that helps people give up smoking.
www.quit.org.uk

Books

Learn to say no: Smoking, Angela Royston (Heinemann Library, 2000)

Need to know: Tobacco, Sean Connolly (Heinemann Library, 2001)

What's at issue: Drugs and you, Bridget Lawless (Heinemann Library, 1999)

World Wide Web

If you want to find out more about **tobacco**, you can search the Internet using keywords like these:

- secondary + smoker
- 'lung cancer'
- drugs
- quit + smoking

You can also find your own keywords by using headings or words from this book. Use the search tips opposite to help you find the most useful websites.

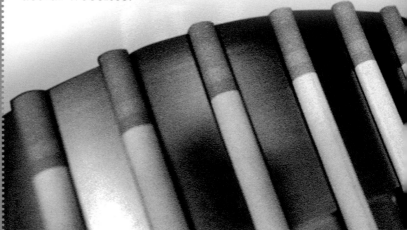

Search tips

There are billions of pages on the Internet so it can be difficult to find exactly what you are looking for. For example, if you just type in 'tobacco' on a search engine like Google, you'll get a list of more than 5.5 million web pages. These search skills will help you find useful websites more quickly:

- Know exactly what you want to find out about first
- Use simple keywords instead of whole sentences
- Use two to six keywords in a search, putting the most important words first
- Be precise – only use names of people, places or things
- If you want to find words that go together, put quote marks around them, for example 'secondary smoker' or 'tobacco addiction'
- Use the advanced section of your search engine.

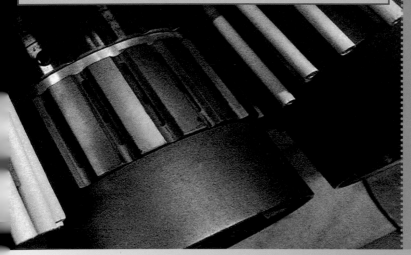

Search engine

A search engine looks through the web and lists the sites that match the words in the search box. They can give thousands of links, but the best matches are at the top of the list, on the first page. Try searching with **www.bbc.co.uk/search**

Search directory

A search directory is like a library of websites. You can search by keyword or subject and browse through the different sites like you would look through books on a library shelf.
A good example is **www.yahooligans.com**

Glossary

acupuncture traditional Chinese treatment using needles

addict someone who finds it difficult or impossible to live without something

addicted unable to live without something

alveoli tiny air sacs in the lungs

amputate cut off

artery tube carrying blood from the heart to other parts of the body

asthma illness that makes breathing very difficult

billion one thousand million

blend mixture

blood pressure pressure of the blood going around the body; high blood pressure is dangerous

carbon monoxide poisonous gas

central nervous system the brain and spinal cord, which carry signals to the rest of the body

charcoal burned wood

compensation money paid to try to make up for something bad that has happened to someone

diabetes disease where sugar and starch are not absorbed into the body properly

efficient good at doing its job

encourage help

erection stiffening and enlarging of the penis when sexually excited

exported sold by one country to another

fertility ability to have children

fragrance smell

gum disease inflammation of the gum and, in bad cases, loss of bone that surrounds the teeth and holds them in place

heart rate speed at which the heart pumps blood around the body

hypnosis sleep-like state that someone puts you into so they can affect the things you think and do

illegal against the law

impotence inability to get an erection

inflammation painful redness or swelling

inhale breathe smoke into your lungs

intestines long tube that carries food from your stomach to your anus

legal allowed by the law

lozenge tablet that dissolves in the mouth

lungs part of the body used for breathing

miscarriage when a pregnancy ends before the unborn baby has developed enough to live

multinational company that operates in several countries

nicotine addictive, colourless chemical that is poisonous in large amounts

non-smoker someone who does not smoke

paranoid very worried

pneumonia serious illness of the lungs that makes it difficult to breathe

pore tiny hole

respiratory related to breathing

sperm special cells produced by male sex organs that join with a female egg to make a new living thing

sponsorship when a company helps to pay for something in return for advertising

still birth giving birth to a baby that has died in the womb

surgery operation in hospital

tar brown, treacle-like substance that contains poisons like arsenic and cyanide

tax-payer person who pays taxes

toxic poisonous

tuberculosis serious disease affecting the lungs, which causes small swellings or lumps to appear

Index